A Collection of Readings

COLLECTION 2/1

Silver Burdett Ginn

299 Jefferson Road, P.O. Box 480

Parsippany, NJ 07054-0480

Acknowledgments appear on page 368, which constitutes an extension of this copyright page.

2000 Printing.

ISBN: 0-663-61220-9   10 11 12 13 14 15 16 17 RRD 02 01 00

LITERATURE WORKS

A Collection of Readings

COLLECTION 2 / 1

THEMES

My Family, Friends, and Neighbors

Nature at Your Door

Stretch Your Imagination

SILVER BURDETT GINN

Parsippany, NJ

Atlanta, GA   Deerfield, IL   Irving, TX   Needham, MA   Upland, CA

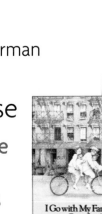

Nature at Your Door

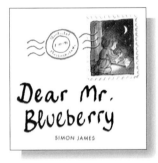

Theme
Trade
Books

Stretch Your Imagination

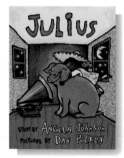

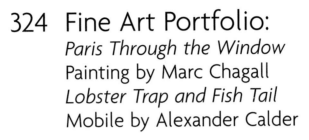

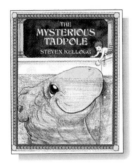

Theme
Trade
Books

My Family, Friends, and Neighbors

Contents

Author and Illustrator at Work

Rebecca C. Jones was sick very often as a child. So she invented imaginary people to keep her company while she was sick. Today, many of these imaginary characters appear in her books. Besides writing books, Rebecca also writes stories and articles for newspapers and magazines.

★ Award-winning Illustrator

Beth Peck makes pictures for many books. She lives in Wisconsin with her husband and young daughter. In *Matthew and Tilly*, she made the pictures look like the neighborhood in New York City where she grew up.

★ Award-winning Book

MATTHEW and TILLY

by REBECCA C. JONES
illustrated by BETH PECK

MATTHEW and TILLY were friends.

They rode bikes together,

and they played hide-and-seek together.

They sold lemonade together. When business was slow,

they played sidewalk games together.

And sometimes they ate ice-cream cones together.

Once they even rescued a lady's kitten
from a tree together.

The lady gave them money
for the bubble-gum machines.

So later they chewed gum together and
remembered how brave they had been.

Sometimes, though, Matthew and Tilly got sick of each other.

One day when they were coloring, Matthew broke Tilly's purple crayon. He didn't mean to, but he did.

"You broke my crayon," Tilly said in her crabbiest voice.

"It was an old crayon," Matthew said in his grouchiest voice. "It was ready to break."

"No, it wasn't," Tilly said. "It was a brand-new crayon, and you broke it. You always break everything."

"Stop being so picky," Matthew said. "You're always so picky and stinky and mean."

"Well, you're so stupid," Tilly said. "You're so stupid and stinky and mean."

Matthew stomped up the stairs.
By himself.

Tilly found a piece of chalk and began
drawing numbers and squares on the sidewalk.
By herself.

Upstairs, Matthew got out his cash register and some cans so he could play store. He piled the cans extra high, and he put prices on everything. This was the best store he had ever made. Probably because that picky and stinky and mean old Tilly wasn't around to mess it up.

But he didn't have a customer. And playing store wasn't much fun without a customer.

Tilly finished drawing the numbers and squares. She drew them really big, with lots of squiggly lines. This was the best sidewalk game she had ever drawn. Probably because that stupid and stinky and mean old Matthew wasn't around to mess it up.

But she didn't have anyone to play with. And a sidewalk game wasn't much fun without another player.

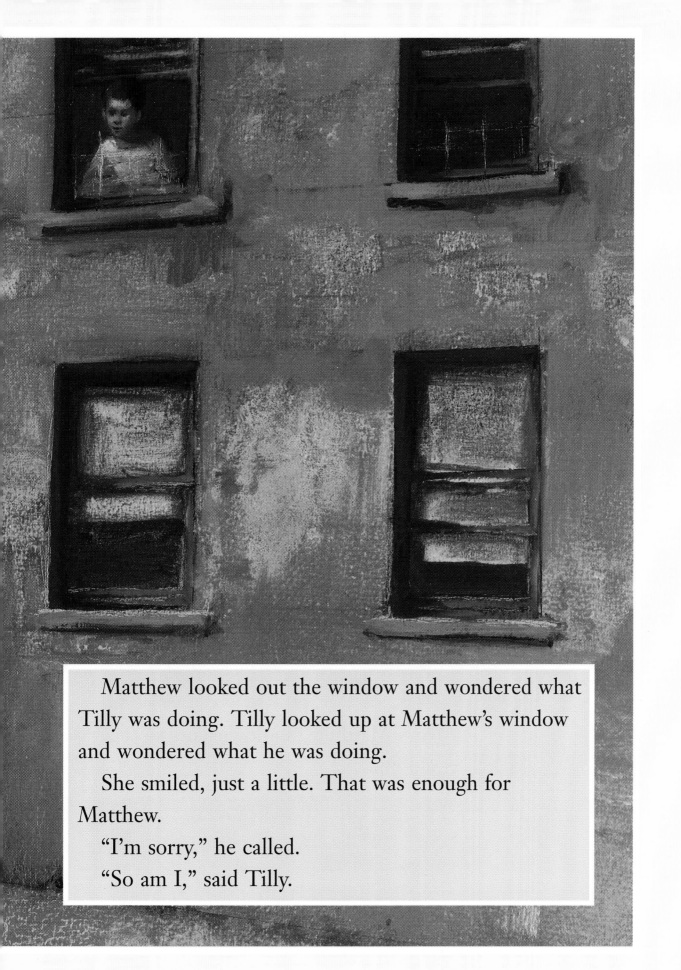

Matthew looked out the window and wondered what Tilly was doing. Tilly looked up at Matthew's window and wondered what he was doing.

She smiled, just a little. That was enough for Matthew.

"I'm sorry," he called.

"So am I," said Tilly.

And Matthew ran downstairs so they could play.

Together again.

In Response

Act Without Words Show what happened when Matthew and Tilly had a fight. Act it out with a partner, without using any words. Just show feelings and actions.

Make a Card What if Matthew and Tilly decided to send cards to each other to end the fight? Make a card for Matthew or Tilly to send. Use words and pictures.

Solve a Problem Think of a time you had a fight with a friend. Draw a picture and write what happened. How did you solve the problem? Share stories with a partner.

Friends

How do you know when you have a friend? Here are some friends in action. They may remind you of someone you know.

A friend is someone who  answers your letters.

"When Andrew went to Florida, he sent us postcards of big alligators he said he wrestled."

Vita Palombo and Amy Travis

A friend is someone who makes you laugh when you're hurting.

"Even though we play on opposite T-ball teams, we cheer each other on. We feel sad when our friend misses the ball. It's awesome when he hits it!"

Cameron Nickless and J.R. Craig

A friend is someone who eats lunch with you on your first day at a new school.

Author and Illustrator at Work

★ Award-winning Author

When **Arnold Lobel** was seven or eight, his teacher sometimes asked him to tell the class a story. He made up his stories on the spot. They were so exciting that the other children in his class screamed and yelled.

When Arnold finished school, his first job was drawing advertisements. Then he decided to draw pictures for children's books. Later, he began writing the words, too. His books about Frog and Toad have won many awards.

★ Award-winning Book

The Letter

from *Frog and Toad Are Friends*

Toad was sitting on his front porch.
Frog came along and said,
"What is the matter, Toad?
You are looking sad."

"Yes," said Toad.
"This is my sad time of day.
It is the time
when I wait for the mail to come.
It always makes me very unhappy."
"Why is that?" asked Frog.
"Because I never get any mail,"
said Toad.

"Not ever?" asked Frog.
"No, never," said Toad.
"No one has ever sent me a letter.
Every day my mailbox is empty.
That is why waiting for the mail
is a sad time for me."
Frog and Toad sat on the porch,
feeling sad together.

Then Frog said,
"I have to go home now, Toad.
There is something that I must do."
Frog hurried home.

He found a pencil
and a piece of paper.
He wrote on the paper.

He put the paper in an envelope.
On the envelope he wrote
"A LETTER FOR TOAD."
Frog ran out of his house.
He saw a snail that he knew.
"Snail," said Frog, "please take
this letter to Toad's house
and put it in his mailbox."
"Sure," said the snail. "Right away."

Then Frog ran back to Toad's house.
Toad was in bed, taking a nap.
"Toad," said Frog,
"I think you should get up
and wait for the mail some more."
"No," said Toad,
"I am tired of waiting for the mail."

Frog looked out of the window
at Toad's mailbox.
The snail was not there yet.
"Toad," said Frog, "you never know
when someone may send you a letter."
"No, no," said Toad. "I do not think
anyone will ever send me a letter."

Frog looked out of the window.
The snail was not there yet.
"But, Toad," said Frog,
"someone may send you a letter today."
"Don't be silly," said Toad.
"No one has ever sent me
a letter before, and no one
will send me a letter today."

Frog looked out of the window.
The snail was still not there.
"Frog, why do you keep looking
out of the window?" asked Toad.
"Because now I am waiting
for the mail," said Frog.
"But there will not be any," said Toad.

"Oh, yes there will," said Frog,
"because I have sent you a letter."
"You have?" said Toad.
"What did you write in the letter?"
Frog said, "I wrote
'Dear Toad, I am glad
that you are my best friend.
Your best friend, Frog.'"

"Oh," said Toad,
"that makes a very good letter."
Then Frog and Toad went out
onto the front porch
to wait for the mail.
They sat there,
feeling happy together.

Frog and Toad waited a long time.
Four days later
the snail got to Toad's house
and gave him the letter from Frog.
Toad was very pleased to have it.

In Response

- **Write to Toad** What would you write in a letter to make Toad feel better? Write a letter to Toad.

- **Picture It** How have you made a friend, someone in your family, or a neighbor feel better? Draw a picture. Show your picture to a partner.

- **T-Shirt Design** Design a T-shirt to cheer up Toad or a friend. Share your T-shirt ideas with others.

Computer
Pen Pals

Frog and Toad spend a lot of time together, but some friends never meet! They are pen pals. Pen pals write letters to each other. Many send their letters in the mail. Others use computers to send their letters. Courtney, age nine, and her sister Meaghan have pen pals in four countries.

Courtney explains how she found her computer pen pals:

1 "My dad showed me how to use e-mail. We put a letter on the kids' news group, and then we sent it out."

2 "It went to every computer in that group. When they checked their messages, they saw it!"

3 "The next day I turned my computer on, and I had a message waiting for me! Every day I get more and more."

60

Courtney's sister Meaghan, who is seven, says:

"Since I started using e-mail, I learned that e-mail is fun. I think I am learning to read more, too. I have a hard time reading my messages sometimes, and Courtney helps me with it."

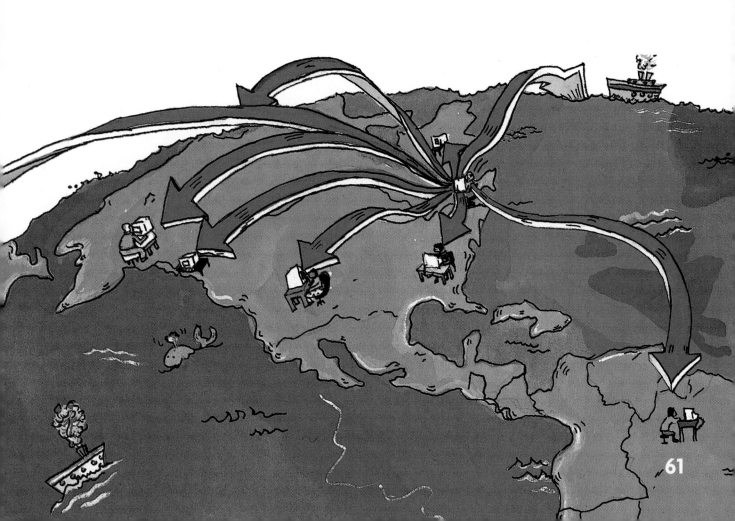

Author and Illustrator at Work

 **Karen Barbour** has written many books. She also makes pictures for books, including the pictures in this story. The idea for this story came to her from a friend she grew up with in Brooklyn, New York. The friend and her family worked in a small Italian restaurant.

Karen likes to travel. She likes to bring her family with her where ever she goes. *Little Nino's Pizzeria* was her first children's book.

★ Award-winning Book

My dad, Nino, makes the best pizza in the world.

I'm his best helper.

I help knead the pizza dough,

I help stir the pizza sauce,

and I help grate the cheese.

When the customers are finished, I know how to pick up
their plates and carry out the dirty dishes.

I help give the extra pizzas to hungry people in the alley
who have no homes.

And . . . I help my dad serve our pizza pies!

People come from all over town to eat at Little Nino's.
They wait in long lines because our restaurant is so small.

One night a man came to see my dad after the last pizza.
What did he want?

That night my dad told my mom we would be making lots
more money now.

The next day, my dad locked up Little Nino's. Soon he
opened a big, fancy, expensive restaurant. He called it
Big Nino.

I tried to help in the dining room. But the waiters tripped over me and spilled a lot of food.

I tried to help in the kitchen, but François the chef pushed me away.

I asked my dad how I could help, but he was too busy to even notice me.

No matter how I tried to be helpful, I was always in the way.

So I went home.

I missed Little Nino's.

But then one night my dad came home from Big Nino
extra-tired. He said . . .

"I miss cutting tomatoes, and chopping onions, and kneading dough. I'm tired of so much paperwork and money talk," he shouted. "I want . . .

I WANT TO MAKE PIZZA!"

And then he looked at me.
"Tony—my best helper!"

So the next day we went back to Little Nino's. Soon we
reopened it, and the man from Big Nino got a new person
to be in charge there.

My dad, Nino, still makes the best pizza in the world.
But he changed the name of our restaurant.

Little Tony's!

In Response

Make a Sign Make a poster or sign advertising Little Tony's Pizzeria. Use words and pictures.

TV Stars Create a television advertisement for Little Tony's. Act it out with classmates. Use drawings, too!

So Many Jobs Tony has many jobs in the pizzeria. Imagine that you work with Tony. Make a list of things you could do, or talk about them with a classmate.

When the Robinsons gather
Just before bed
The kids in pajamas
The homework's been read
It's time for the family
To have some fun
"It's fambly time!"
Says the littlest one

Fambly Time

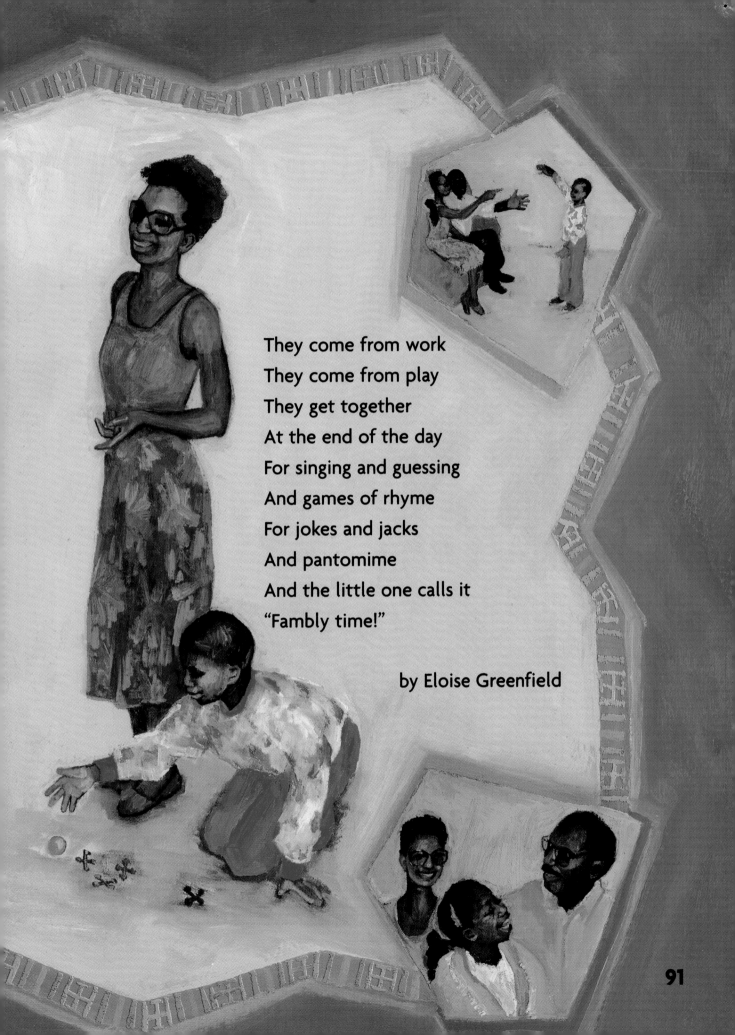

They come from work
They come from play
They get together
At the end of the day
For singing and guessing
And games of rhyme
For jokes and jacks
And pantomime
And the little one calls it
"Fambly time!"

by Eloise Greenfield

Looking at Families

Older people add a lot to children's lives. What do you think the boy is learning during this banjo lesson? What special time does this remind *you* of?

The Banjo Lesson
Painting by Henry O. Tanner (U.S.), 1893

Look at the children's faces in this painting. What are they thinking as they listen to the story? Do you have a favorite story that you would like Mrs. Cassatt to read to you?

Mrs. Cassatt Reading to Her Grandchildren
Painting by Mary Cassatt (U.S.), 1880

Author and Illustrator at Work

 **Pat Mora** grew up in El Paso, Texas, near Mexico. She speaks both English and Spanish. She remembered her childhood when she wrote this story.

 **Cecily Lang** loved to make collages when she was young. She didn't think she was good at art in school, however, because she couldn't stay inside the lines.

A Birthday Basket for Tía

by Pat Mora ▾ illustrated by Cecily Lang

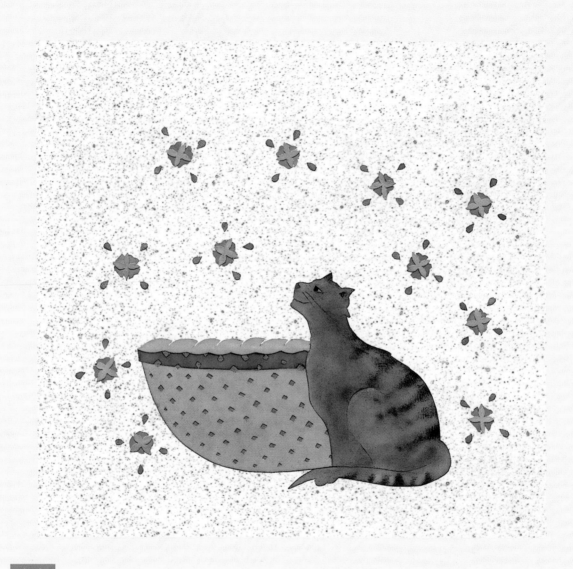

Today is secret day. I curl my cat into my arms and say, "Ssshh, Chica. Can you keep our secret, silly cat?"

Today is special day. Today is my great-aunt's ninetieth birthday. Ten, twenty, thirty, forty, fifty, sixty, seventy, eighty, ninety. Ninety years old. *¡Noventa años!*

At breakfast Mamá asks, "What is today, Cecilia?" I say, "Special day. Birthday day."

Mamá is cooking for the surprise party. I smell beans bubbling on the stove. Mamá is cutting fruit—pineapple, watermelon, mangoes. I sit in the backyard and watch Chica chase butterflies. I hear bees bzzzzz.

I draw pictures in the sand with a stick. I draw a picture of my aunt, my *Tía*. I say, "Chica, what will we give Tía?"

Chica and I walk around the front yard and the backyard looking for a good present. We walk around the house. We look in Mamá's room. We look in my closet and drawers.

I say, "Chica, shall we give her my little pots, my piggy bank, my tin fish, my dancing puppet?"

I say, "Mamá, can Chica and I use this basket?"
Mamá asks, "Why, Cecilia?" "It's a surprise for the
surprise party," I answer.

Chica jumps into the basket. "No," I say. "Not for
you, silly cat. This is a birthday basket for Tía."

I put a book in the basket. When Tía comes to
our house, she reads it to me. It's our favorite book.
I sit close to her on the sofa. I smell her perfume.
Sometimes Chica tries to read with us. She sits on
the book. I say, "Silly cat. Books are not for sitting."

I put Tía's favorite mixing bowl on the book in the
basket. Tía and I like to make *bizcochos*, sugary cookies
for the family. Tía says, "Cecilia, help me stir the cookie
dough." She says, "Cecilia, help me roll the cookie
dough." When we take the warm cookies from the oven,
Tía says, "Cecilia, you are a very good cook."

I put a flowerpot in the mixing bowl on the book
in the basket. Tía and I like to grow flowers for the
kitchen window. Chica likes to put her face in the
flowers. "Silly cat," I say.

I put a teacup in the flowerpot that is in the
mixing bowl on the book in the basket. When I'm sick,
my aunt makes me hot mint tea, *hierbabuena*. She
brings it to me in bed. She brings me a cookie too.

I put a red ball in the teacup that is in the flowerpot in the mixing bowl on the book in the basket. On warm days Tía sits outside and throws me the ball.

She says, "Cecilia, when I was a little girl in Mexico, my sisters and I played ball. We all wore long dresses and had long braids."

Chica and I go outside. I pick flowers to decorate
Tía's basket. On summer days when I am swinging high
up to the sky, Tía collects flowers for my room.

Mamá calls, "Cecilia, where are you?"

Chica and I run and hide our surprise.

I say, "Mamá, can you find the birthday basket for Tía?"

Mamá looks under the table. She looks in the refrigerator. She looks under my bed. She asks, "Chica, where is the birthday basket?"

Chica rubs against my closet door. Mamá and I laugh. I show her my surprise.

After my nap, Mamá and I fill a piñata with candy. We fill the living room with balloons. I hum, mmmmm, a little work song like the one Tía hums when she sets the table or makes my bed. I help Mamá set the table with flowers and tiny cakes.

"Here come the musicians," says Mamá. I open the front door. Our family and friends begin to arrive too.

I curl Chica into my arms. Then Mamá says, "Sshh, here comes Tía."

I rush to open the front door. "Tía! Tía!" I shout. She hugs me and says, "Cecilia, *¿qué pasa?* What is this?"

"SURPRISE!" we all shout. "¡*Feliz cumpleaños!* Happy
birthday!" The musicians begin to play their guitars and violins.

"Tía! Tía!" I say. "It's special day, birthday day! It's your ninetieth birthday surprise party!" Tía and I laugh.

I give her the birthday basket. Everyone gets close to see what's inside. Slowly Tía smells the flowers. She looks at me and smiles. Then she takes the red ball out of the teacup and the teacup out of the flowerpot.

She pretends to take a sip of tea and we all laugh.

Carefully, Tía takes the flowerpot out of the bowl and the bowl off of the book. She doesn't say a word. She just stops and looks at me. Then she takes our favorite book out of the basket.

And guess who jumps into the basket?

Chica. Everyone laughs.

    Then the music starts and my aunt surprises me.
She takes my hands in hers. Without her cane, she starts
to dance with me.

In Response

 Tell a Friend Cecilia put many special things in the birthday basket for Tía. What would you like to get in a birthday basket? Share your ideas with a partner.

 Birthday Baskets What would Matthew or Tilly like to get in a birthday basket? What would Frog, Toad, or Tony want? Draw a birthday basket for one of these characters.

 Party Time What would you do at a special birthday party for a good friend? Act out your ideas with a partner.

Zuni Grandmother
A traditional Zuni poem

Grandmother of mine
how have you been passing the days?
Happily, our child
surely I could be grandmother
to anyone
for we
have the whole village as our children

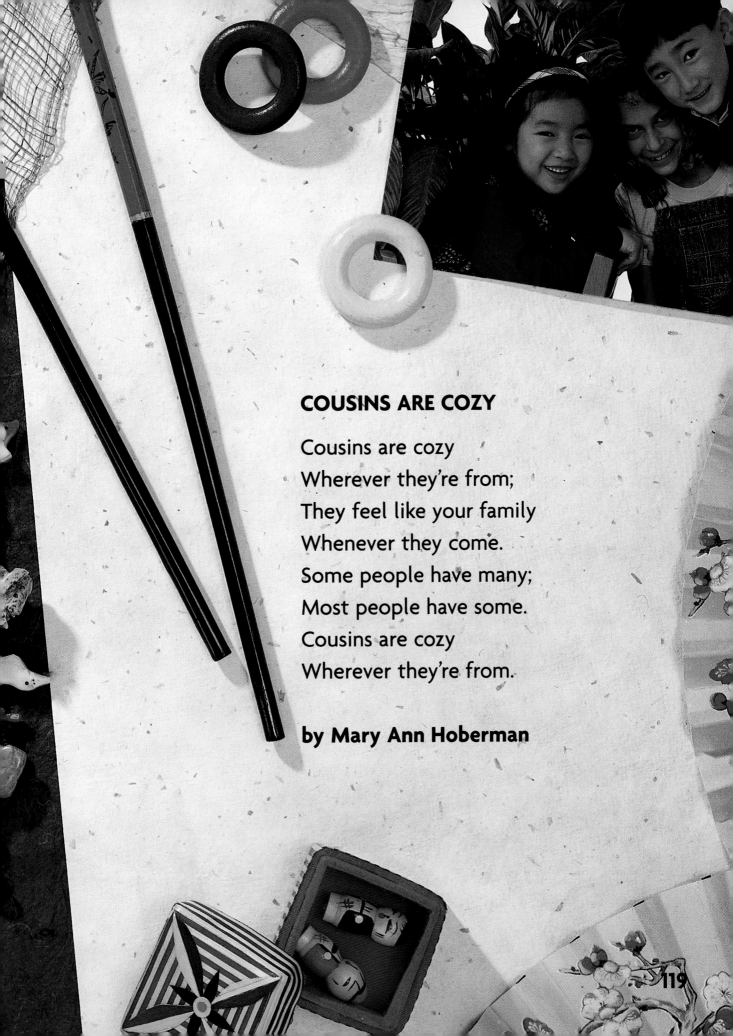

COUSINS ARE COZY

Cousins are cozy
Wherever they're from;
They feel like your family
Whenever they come.
Some people have many;
Most people have some.
Cousins are cozy
Wherever they're from.

by **Mary Ann Hoberman**

The Terrible Thing that Happened at Our House

by Marge Blaine, illustrated by John C. Wallner, Four Winds Press, 1975

When her mother goes back to work, a young girl finds her family life in complete disorder. What will it take to have things the way they used to be?

Clean Your Room, Harvey Moon!

by Pat Cummings, Bradbury Press, 1991

Harvey's room is a mess. His mother won't let him watch Saturday cartoons until the room is clean. Harvey meets the mess head on—and finds a place for everything!

Six-Dinner Sid

by Inga Moore, Simon & Schuster, 1991

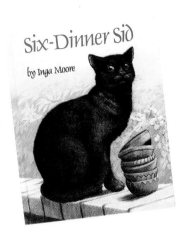

Unknown to the people on Aristotle Street, Sid the cat is the pet for six different owners. Life is perfect for Sid—six dinners a day—until Sid gets sick.

Miss Tizzy

by Libba Moore Gray, illustrated by Jada
Rowland, Simon & Schuster, 1993
The children in the neighborhood love
Miss Tizzy. She does so many nice
things for them, like baking cookies
and making puppets. When Miss Tizzy
gets sick, the children return her love
in special ways.

Climbing Kansas Mountains

by George Shannon, illustrated by Thomas
B. Allen, Bradbury Press, 1993
Sam and his father set out one
afternoon to climb a Kansas
mountain. Even though Sam knows
Kansas is flat, he and his dad find
their own special mountain.

Nature at Your Door

Contents

Author and Illustrator at Work

 Shelley Rotner's dad took pictures of her all the time when she was a little girl. He also taught her to use a camera. When Shelley needs help with a book she is writing, she reads it out loud to her daughter, who is nine.

 **Ken Kreisler** and Shelley Rotner like to work together on books that help children understand nature. Some of the first books Ken liked were books that had photos of the ocean. Today he works for a boat magazine.

★ Award-winning Book

NATURE SPY

written by SHELLEY ROTNER and KEN KREISLER
photographs by SHELLEY ROTNER

AWARD
WINNER

I like to go outside—to look around and discover things.

To take a really close look, even closer

and closer.

My mother says I'm a curious kid. She calls me a nature spy.

Sometimes I look so closely, I can see the lines on a shiny green leaf,

or one small acorn on a branch,

or seeds in a pod.

I notice the feathers of a bird,

or the golden eye of a frog.

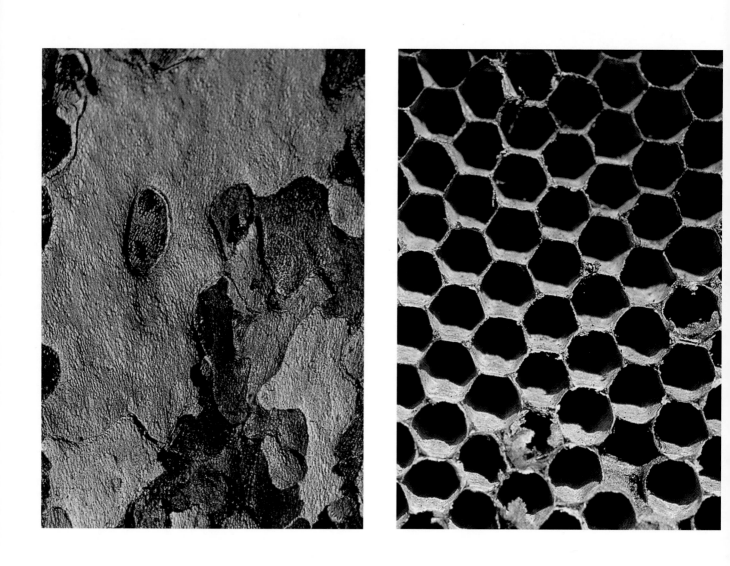

When you look closely, things look so different—
like the bark of a tree or an empty hornet's nest,

the seeds of a sunflower, or even a rock.

Sometimes there's a pattern, like ice on a frozen pond,

or a spider's web, or a butterfly's wing.

 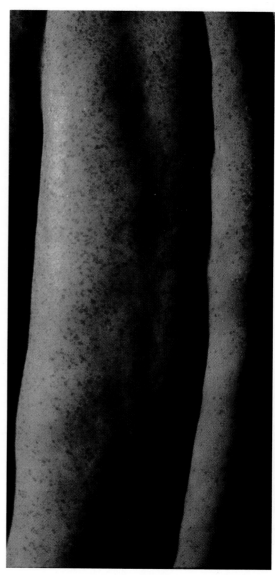

Everything has its own shape, color,

and size.

Look closely at a turtle's shell,

or a dog's fur,

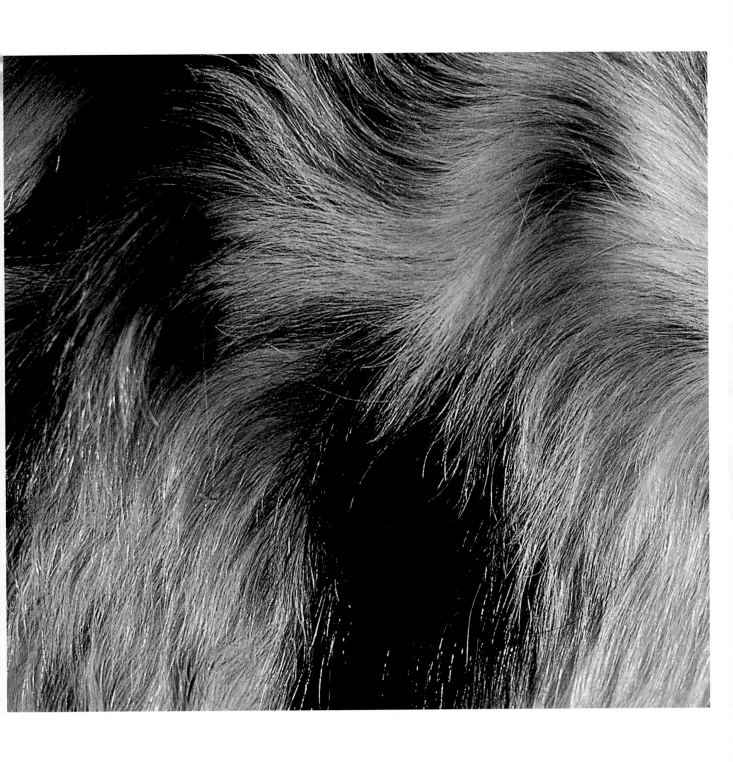

or even raspberries,

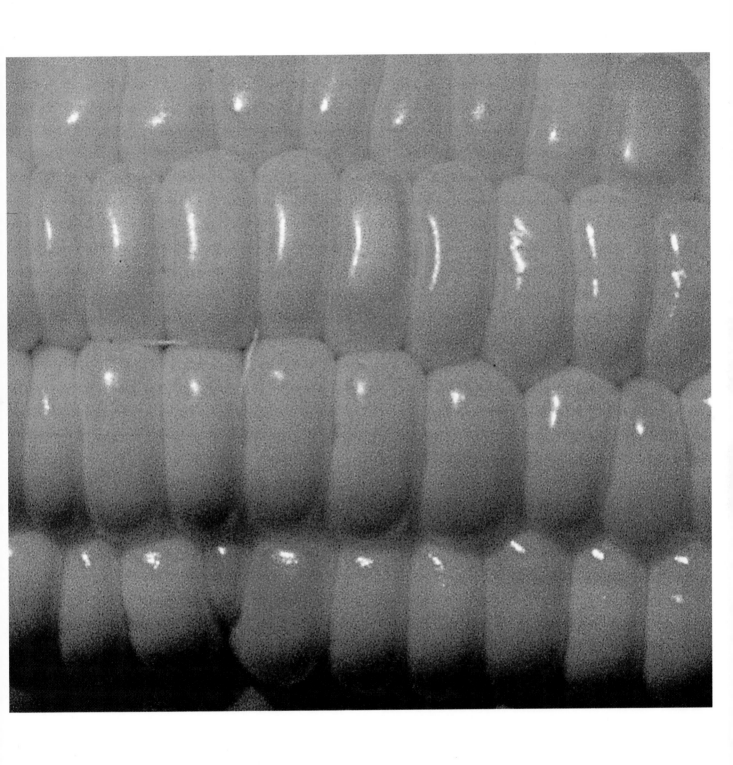

or kernels of corn.

No matter where you look, up, down

or all around,

there's always something to see when you're a nature spy!

IN RESPONSE

Spy on Nature Be a nature spy. With a partner, look out a window in your classroom. Tell each other what you see.

Nature Writing Look closely at plants, animals, or objects in your classroom. What do you see, feel, or hear? Draw and write about what you spy.

Nature Drawing Make a poster about how to be a nature spy. List five things that make someone a great nature spy.

Looking at Animals

Gregorio Marzán makes sculptures of animals he has seen in New York and Puerto Rico. His sculptures, like the dog below, are made of bits and pieces of things he finds.

Lulu Yazzie is a Navajo artist. She makes animal sculptures out of cottonwood – a kind of tree found near her home in Arizona.

What is fun about these two sculptures? How do these artists feel about nature?

Dachshund
Sculpture by Gregorio Marzán (Puerto Rican), early 1980s

Rooster
Sculpture by Lulu Yazzie (U.S.), 1990

Looking Around

Bees
   own the clover,
birds
   own the sky,
rabbits,
   the meadow
   with low grass and high.

Frogs
   own the marshes,
ants
   own the ground . . .
   I hope they don't mind
   my looking around.

by Aileen Fisher

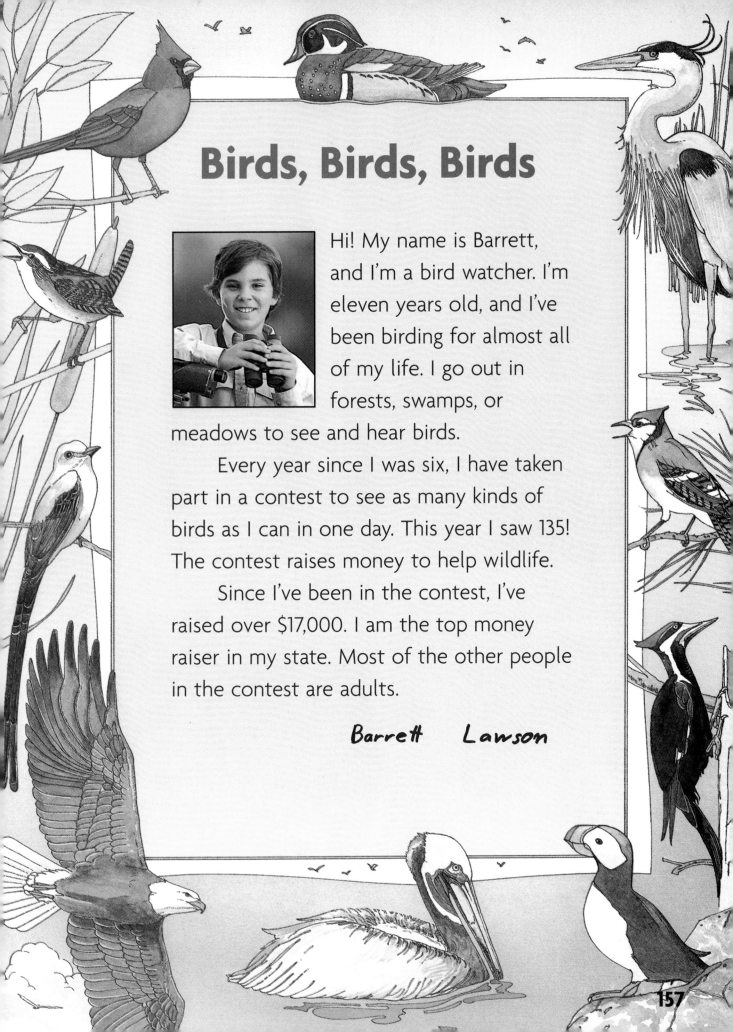

Birds, Birds, Birds

Hi! My name is Barrett, and I'm a bird watcher. I'm eleven years old, and I've been birding for almost all of my life. I go out in forests, swamps, or meadows to see and hear birds.

Every year since I was six, I have taken part in a contest to see as many kinds of birds as I can in one day. This year I saw 135! The contest raises money to help wildlife.

Since I've been in the contest, I've raised over $17,000. I am the top money raiser in my state. Most of the other people in the contest are adults.

Barrett   Lawson

Author and Illustrator at Work

This book took **Jeannie Baker** two years to make. She spent ten months in New York City looking at buildings and people. Then she used rocks, chips of old paint, grass, leaves, hair, cloth, and clay to make the pictures. The people in this story have hair made of real hair. They have clothes made of real cloth. Jeannie also likes to include weeds and models of old buildings in her pictures.

★ Award-winning Book

Home in the Sky
by Jeannie Baker

Every day, at sunrise and sunset,
the pigeons burst into the sky.

The pigeons belong to Mike
and live on the roof
of an abandoned, burned-out building.
He built their coop from scrap lumber
found in the neighborhood.
Werewulf, Mike's dog, lives in the building
and guards the birds.

One morning, before feeding time,
Mike flies his pigeons as usual.

When Mike whistles, they know
it is time to come back for their food.
All the pigeons fly home,
except Light, who flies away.

After a while Light is very hungry.
He joins some street pigeons
who have found food.
But when Light tries to eat,
they screech, peck, and snatch
the food from him.

Light flies on. . . .
It starts to rain.
His wings become heavy.

He flies through an open doorway.
The doors close behind him.
He is in a train.

A boy picks him up, holding him firmly so he will feel safe, and gently strokes his feathers.

175

The boy walks home
cuddling Light to his chest.

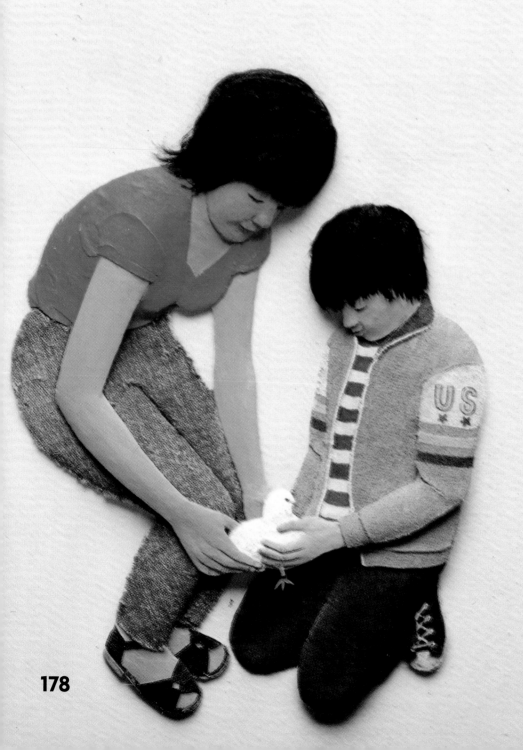

He wants to keep the pigeon,
but his mother explains
that the band around Light's leg
means that he belongs to someone.

The boy places Light
on an outside windowsill
hoping he will stay.
But Light spreads his wings
and flies away.

Instinct tells Light
where to go.
He flies high over
unfamiliar buildings.

183

That evening,
as Mike is feeding his pigeons,
Light lands on his shoulder
and nestles against his face.

On his roof the next morning,
the boy eyes a flock of pigeons flying
in sweeping curves across the sky.
He is sure he sees a white pigeon
among them.

In Response

Find New Things Every time you look at the pictures in this story, you can see new things. Look at the pictures closely. What new things do you see? Tell a friend.

Draw Your School Light flew many places. Draw a picture of what your school and playground could look like to a pigeon in the sky above.

Secret Message Light is a homing pigeon. Write a note that the boy could have written for Light to carry back to Mike.

BUDDIES

A boy and a bird can be buddies

not the kind who run

in the sunshine together

or gather for games of sport

but buddies of another sort

who meet just at mealtimes maybe

and trust

by Eloise Greenfield

PAINT BY MR AMOS FERGUSON

Simon James lives in Devon, England. He has had many jobs in his life. He has been a police officer, a farmworker, and an artist. He wrote the story and also drew the pictures for *Dear Mr. Blueberry*. He made the lines in the pictures with black ink. He used watercolors to add color between the lines. Simon thinks children should enjoy art and have fun making a mess.

★ Award-winning Book

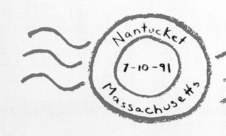

Dear Mr. Blueberry

SIMON JAMES

Dear Mr. Blueberry,

　I love whales very much and I think I saw one in my pond today. Please send me some information on whales, as I think he might be hurt.

Love
Emily

Dear Emily,

Here are some details about whales. I don't think you'll find it was a whale you saw, because whales don't live in ponds, but in salt water.

Yours sincerely
Your teacher,

Mr. Blueberry

Dear Mr. Blueberry,

    I am now putting salt into the pond every day before breakfast and last night I saw my whale smile. I think he is feeling better.

    Do you think he might be lost?

Love
Emily

Dear Emily,

Please don't put any more salt in the pond. I'm sure your parents won't be pleased.

I'm afraid there can't be a whale in your pond, because whales don't get lost, they always know where they are in the oceans.

Yours sincerely,

Mr. Blueberry

Dear Mr. Blueberry,

   Tonight I am very happy because I saw my whale jump up and spurt lots of water. He looked blue.

   Does this mean he might be a blue whale?

Love
Emily

P.S. What can I feed him with?

Dear Emily,

    Blue whales are blue and they eat tiny shrimplike creatures that live in the sea. However, I must tell you that a blue whale is much too big to live in your pond.

    Yours sincerely,

    Mr. Blueberry

P.S. Perhaps it is a blue goldfish?

Dear Mr. Blueberry,

Last night I read your letter to my whale. Afterward he let me stroke his head. It was very exciting.

I secretly took him some crunched-up cornflakes and bread crumbs. This morning I looked in the pond and they were all gone!

I think I shall call him Arthur. What do you think?

Love
Emily

Dear Emily,

    I must point out to you quite forcibly now that in no way could a whale live in your pond. You may not know that whales are migratory, which means they travel great distances each day.

    I am sorry to disappoint you.

Yours sincerely,

Mr. Blueberry

Dear Mr. Blueberry,

Tonight I'm a little sad. Arthur
has gone. I think your letter made
sense to him and he has decided
to be migratory again.

Love
Emily

Dear Emily,

Please don't be too sad, it really was impossible for a whale to live in your pond. Perhaps when you are older you would like to sail the oceans studying and protecting whales.

Yours sincerely,

Mr. Blueberry

Dear Mr. Blueberry,

It's been the happiest day! I
went to the beach and you'll never
guess, but I saw Arthur! I called to
him and he smiled. I knew it was
Arthur because he let me stroke
his head.

I gave him some of my
sandwich . . .

and then we said good-bye.

I shouted that I loved him very much and, I hope you don't mind, I said you loved him, too.

Love
Emily (and Arthur)

Whale Talk If the whale could talk, what would it say? How do you think the whale feels when Emily pours salt in the water and feeds it cornflakes? Talk about your ideas with a partner, and then act out the ideas together.

Write to Emily If Emily wrote these letters to you, what would you write back? Answer one or two of Emily's letters. Show your letters to a friend.

Whales Ahead Make a whale like the one in the story. Use clay or crayons and paper. Show your whale to others.

If You Ever

If you ever ever ever ever ever,
  If you ever ever ever meet a whale,
You must never never never never never,
  You must never never never touch its tail:
For if you ever ever ever ever ever,
  If you ever ever ever touch its tail,
You will never never never never never,
  You will never never meet another whale.

Anonymous

216

Theme Trade Books

Fish Fish Fish

by Georgie Adams, illustrated by
Brigitte Willgoss, Silver Burdett
Ginn, 1996

This book tells you about all
kinds of fish and shows the
many places fish live
underwater—in seas and
oceans and rivers and ponds.
You will see fish with different
shapes and colors, some with
spots and some with stripes.

Arthur's Camp-Out

by Lillian Hoban, Silver Burdett Ginn,
1996

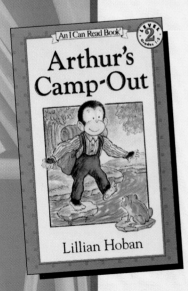

Arthur decides to go on an over-
night field trip to collect things.
First, he falls into brook, then into a
sticker bush. He is scared by a
snake and chased by bats. When it
comes time to camp, Arthur
realizes he has lost all his supplies.
Now what will he do ?

More Books for You to Enjoy

Quiet, Please

by Eve Merriam, illustrated by Sheila Hamanaka, Simon & Schuster, 1993

There are many things you can enjoy during quiet times and peaceful moments, from a tiny breeze to the bark on a birch tree.

River Day

by Jane B. Mason, illustrated by Henri Sorensen, Macmillan, 1994

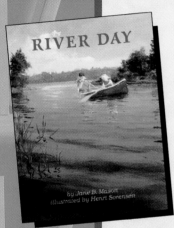

Alex and her grandfather go out on a canoe trip. They share a special time together, observing the water, the fish, and even a giant eagle.

Turtle in July

by Marilyn Singer, illustrated by Jerry Pinkney, Macmillan, 1989

Read about a deer in the snow, a bear waking up in the spring, a cow munching on summer grass. This book of poems explains how different animals react to the seasons.

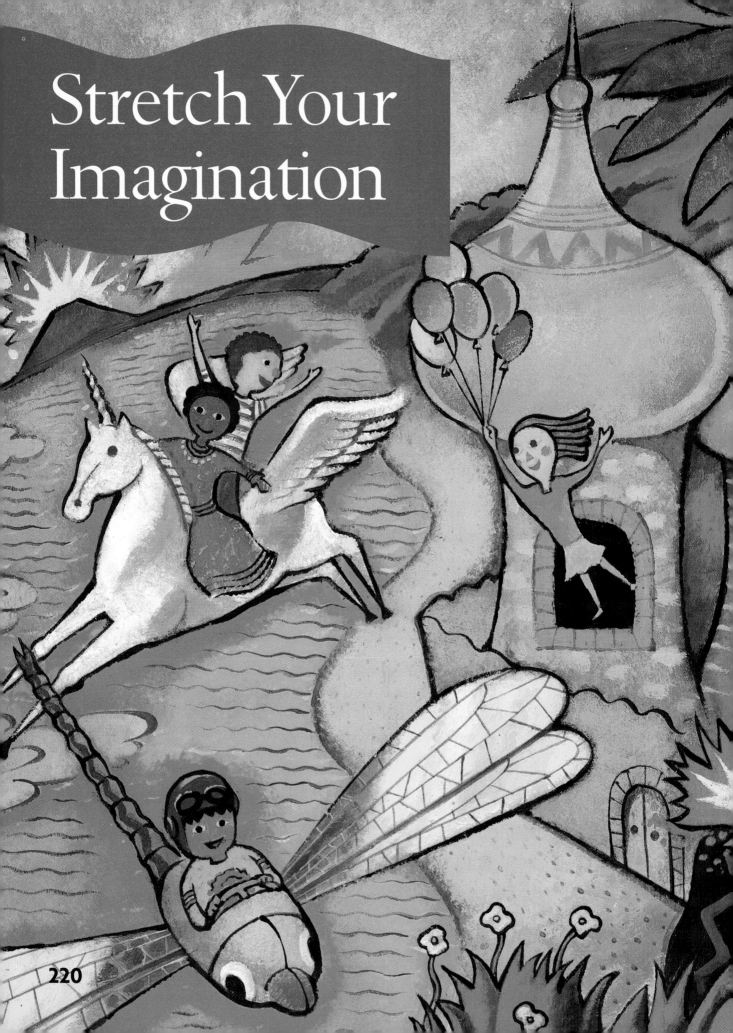

Stretch Your Imagination

Contents

Author and Illustrator at Work

Angela Johnson says that listening to her teacher read stories out loud after lunch was one of the magic times of her life. "Book people came to life. They sat beside me in Maple Grove School." That was when Angela decided to become a writer.

Many children send **Dav Pilkey** pictures they have drawn. He says he often gets ideas from their drawings.

★ Award-winning Book

Maya's granddaddy lived in Alabama, but wintered in Alaska.

He told Maya that was the reason he liked
ice cubes in his coffee.

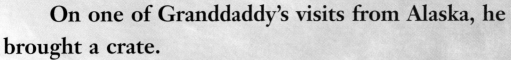

On one of Granddaddy's visits from Alaska, he brought a crate.

A surprise for Maya!

"Something that will teach you fun and sharing." Granddaddy smiled. "Something for my special you."

226

Maya hoped it was a horse or an older brother.
She'd always wanted one or the other.

But it was a pig.

A big pig.
An Alaskan pig, who did a polar bear
imitation and climbed out of the crate.

Julius had come.

Maya's parents didn't think that they would
like Julius.
He showed them no fun, no sharing.

Maya loved Julius, though, so he stayed.

There never was enough food in the house after Julius came to stay.

He slurped coffee and ate too much peanut butter.

He would roll himself in flour when he
wanted Maya to bake him cookies.

Julius made big messes and spread the newspaper
everywhere before anyone could read it.

He left crumbs on the sheets and never
picked up his towels.

Julius made too much noise.
He'd stay up late watching old movies,

and he'd always play records when everybody
else wanted to read.

But Maya knew the other Julius too. . . .

The Julius who was fun to take on walks
'cause he did great dog imitations and chased cats.

The Julius who sneaked into stores with her
and tried on clothes.
    Julius liked anything blue and stretchy.

They'd try on hats too.
Maya liked red felt.
Julius liked straw—it tasted better.

Trying on shoes was hard, though. . . .

Julius would swing for hours on the playground with Maya.

He'd protect her from the scary things at
night too . . . sometimes.

Maya loved the Julius who taught her how
to dance to jazz records . . .

and eat peanut butter from the jar, without getting any on the ceiling.

Maya didn't think all the older brothers in the world could have taught her that.

Julius loved the Maya who taught him that even though he was a pig he didn't have to act like he lived in a barn.

Julius didn't think all the Alaskan pigs in the world could have taught him that.

Maya shared the things she'd learned from
Julius with her friends.
Swinging . . .

trying on hats, and dancing to jazz records.

Julius shared the things Maya had taught
him with her parents . . . sometimes.

And that was all right, because living with
Maya and sharing everything was even better
than being a cool pig from Alaska.

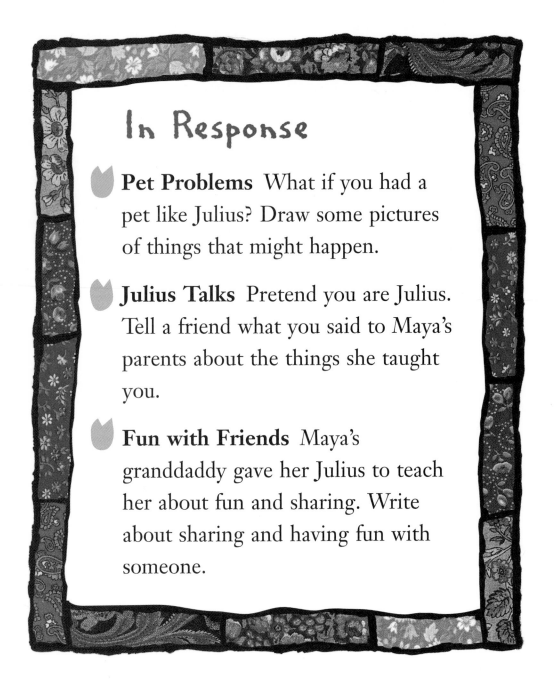

In Response

Pet Problems What if you had a pet like Julius? Draw some pictures of things that might happen.

Julius Talks Pretend you are Julius. Tell a friend what you said to Maya's parents about the things she taught you.

Fun with Friends Maya's granddaddy gave her Julius to teach her about fun and sharing. Write about sharing and having fun with someone.

Pig Tales

In Connecticut, two sisters, Meredith and Rachel Bogue, have a pet pig named Cosmos. Here are our questions about him—and their answers.

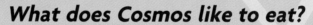

Where does Cosmos live?
In his house in the backyard. When it's really cold, he stays in our house. When he was little, he had a place called the pig-o-minium, under the kitchen counter. Now he has most of the couch.

What does Cosmos like to eat?
He likes dog food, Mom's tomatoes, and Dad's grapes. He loves maple leaves, wallpaper, and parts of the kitchen floor.

How does he act indoors?
He watches TV. He tears up papers and spreads them around. He rolls up rugs with his nose. Then he unrolls them.

How is a pet pig different from a dog?
It's hard taking walks with a pig because so many people stop to ask about him!

Author and Illustrator at Work

Jama Kim Rattigan had many aunts—and uncles—when she was growing up. Her mother was one of twelve children. She says there were good things and bad things about having many aunts. She has shown some good and bad things in this story. Jama lives in Hawaii.

G. Brian Karas likes to draw pictures that make readers feel a certain way. He hopes his pictures will make readers feel happy, sad, or scared.

At eleven o'clock a package arrived for Truman. It was a birthday present from Aunt Fran. Truman looked at the box. It was not moving. He gently picked it up. It felt empty. He turned it over, then smelled it. Presents from Aunt Fran had to be handled very carefully.

Truman slowly opened the box. It was empty! No, there were two cards. The yellow one said: "Happy Birthday dear Truman! I am giving you the ant farm you wanted. Love, your charming Aunt Fran."

The green one said: "Mail this card right away to receive your free ants! Watch them work! Watch them play! Watch them eat! Live ants!"

Truman mailed his card right away. Oh boy. Live ants!
Live ants for his very own!

But he didn't get ants. He got *aunts*.

It was true. There were aunts everywhere. They all loved Truman and made such a fuss!

"My, how you've grown," said Aunt Lulu.

"Isn't he handsome?" said Aunt Jodie.

"Looks just like me," said Aunt Ramona. And they hugged him, and patted his head, and pinched his cheeks, and talked his ears off.

Dear Charming Aunt Fran,

Thank you for the birthday present.
I have fifty-something aunts at my house now.
More are arriving daily. What shall I do?

Love,
Your bug-loving nephew, Truman

P.S. What should I feed the aunts?

Truman looked out his front window. A long, long line of aunts was waiting to get in. They brought their knitting and homemade banana bread and gave Truman more than one hundred-something gift subscriptions to children's magazines.

"Help!" yelled Truman.

"Letter for you," said the postman.

My dear Truman,

I am glad you liked the present. Don't let those ants bug you. Do you have any friends who would like some ants?

Love,
Your clever Aunt Fran

P.S. Feed the ants ant food.

Since they were *his* aunts he wanted them to be good aunts. What was the best aunt food? Not coffee, the aunts stayed up all night. Not alphabet soup, the aunts talked too much. Certainly not chocolate, the aunts kissed him all the time.

So Truman fed them rice pudding for breakfast, jelly sandwiches for lunch, and little hot dogs for supper.

Every morning, all the aunts lined up for inspection. Truman walked up and down the ranks. He looked over each aunt from head to toe. They were ready to get to work.

The aunts got water and sun and fresh air. They blew
bubbles, flew kites, and found birds' nests. Aunt Amy could
do back flips with her eyes closed.

The aunts were strong and happy. They were charming and clever. They slept, played, sang, danced, and talked just enough.

Dear clever Aunt Fran,

I have around two hundred-something aunts now.
I love them all. More aunts keep coming and coming.
They are the best in the world.

Love,
Your aunt-loving nephew, Truman

Yes, they were very good aunts. But they weren't really *his* aunts. And he was running out of room. Could he give them away? Who might want them?

Truman put up a sign:

TRUMAN'S
AUNT
FARM

LIVE AUNTS!
WATCH THEM WORK!
WATCH THEM PLAY!
WATCH THEM EAT!
FREE TO GOOD HOMES

Truman looked out his front window. A long, long line of boys and girls was waiting to get in.

"I want a funny aunt," said one girl, "one who knows jokes and stories."

"I want my aunt to do cartwheels," said a little boy, "and not cry if she falls down and gets dirty."

"Make mine lumpy and soft. A good cuddler," said another boy.

Truman let all the boys and girls in. They looked over the aunts from head to toe. They watched the aunts work and play. They watched the aunts eat. The aunts could tickle, tell stories, do headstands, and roller skate. When the children talked, the aunts really listened. They didn't pat heads, pinch cheeks, or talk ears off. But they still hugged.

Soon, each child found just the right aunt.

"Goodbye, dear Truman!" called the aunts.
"Thanks for a tiptop time."

Truman was sad to see the aunts go. He watched them tiptoe away. He was glad those boys and girls got their own aunts, but something was missing.

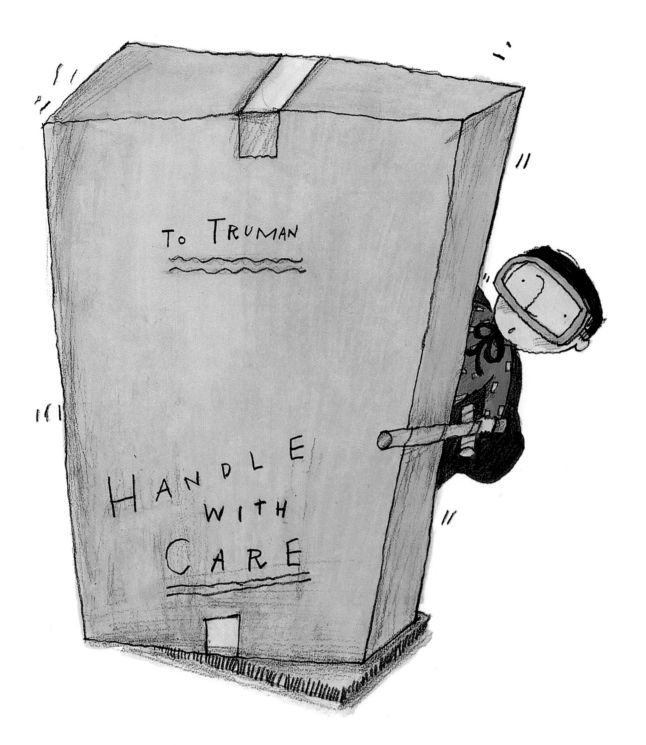

At eleven o'clock the next day another package arrived. Truman looked at the box. It was moving. He tried to pick it up. It was too heavy. He smelled it. It smelled like roses. Carefully, he opened the lid.

Out jumped Aunt Fran!

"Surprise!" She gave Truman a big hug. "But where are your ants?" she said. "I wanted to see them."

"Oh, Aunt Fran! The aunts are gone. They have their own nieces and nephews now."

Aunt Fran put her arm around Truman. He saw the twinkle in her eye. "You did a wonderful thing," said Aunt Fran. "Let's celebrate your birthday."

Truman and his very own Aunt Fran shared a special
day. They had rice pudding for breakfast, jelly sandwiches for
lunch, and little hot dogs for supper. They even had a tickle
contest, but they were too full to do headstands.

IN RESPONSE!

♥ **Write to Aunt Fran** Maybe Aunt Fran never knew that Truman got aunts instead of ants! Pretend you are Truman. Write Aunt Fran another letter to make sure she understands.

♥ **Aunts or Uncles** What would you do if you were sent a hundred aunts or uncles? Show a friend how you would act and what you would do.

♥ **Ant Farm Fun** What might Truman have liked about having an ant farm? Make a list of the things that would be fun about it. Read your list to a friend.

Why Ants Live Everywhere

A folk tale from Burma, retold by Maria Leach

All the animals in the forest were going along, on their way to honor the king of the beasts, King Lion.

The ant was among them. He too was going to bow before the king.

It was a hard journey for him. He had to walk over every leaf and stone in the forest.

The big animals could leap over things, but the ant had to walk up one side and down the other of everything in the way.

When the little ant arrived—LAST—to bow before King Lion, all the animals laughed at him and drove him away.

The ant went back and told the king of the ants that he had tried to honor King Lion and been driven away and laughed at.

So the ant king sent a worm to go crawl in the lion's ear and bite him.

The lion roared. He rolled. He nearly went crazy; but he could not get the tormenting thing out of his ear.

All the animals came running to help him; but
not one of them could reach the worm.

At last the lion sent a message to the king of
the ants.

"Please send someone," he begged, "to crawl
into my ear and pull out this terrible thing."

So the king of the ants sent one of his many
people to go tell the worm, "Come out of the
lion's ear."

The ant arrived. The lion lay moaning with his chin on his paws. The ant walked up the lion's shoulder. He nearly got lost in the thick tawny mane.

But at last he walked into the ear and told the worm, "All right, you can come on out now."

The lion then said that ants had better live everywhere.

Today all the other animals live in their own special places in the world. But ants live everywhere.

Author and Illustrator at Work

Arthur Dorros likes animals. When he was young, he had thirteen box turtles. He called them all Bobby because he couldn't tell them apart. Arthur has always loved to read. When he was young, he read almost a book a day!

When **Elisa Kleven** was young, she turned her closet into a tiny dollhouse. Socks and nutshells became rugs and cradles in the world she created.

★ Award-winning Book

Abuela

by Arthur Dorros

illustrated by Elisa Kleven

$\mathcal{A}$buela takes me on the bus.
We go all around the city.
Abuela is my grandma.
She is my mother's mother.
Abuela means "grandma" in Spanish.

Abuela speaks mostly Spanish because
that's what people spoke where she grew up,
before she came to this country.
Abuela and I are always going places.

Today we're going to the park.
"El parque es lindo," says Abuela.
I know what she means.
I think the park is beautiful too.

"*Tantos pájaros,*" Abuela says
as a flock of birds surrounds us.
So many birds.
They're picking up the bread we brought.

What if they picked me up,
and carried me
high above the park?
What if I could fly?
Abuela would wonder where I was.
Swooping like a bird, I'd call to her.

Then she'd see me flying.
Rosalba the bird.
"Rosalba el pájaro," she'd say.
"Ven, Abuela. Come, Abuela," I'd say.
"Sí, quiero volar," Abuela would reply
as she leaped into the sky
with her skirt flapping in the wind.

We would fly all over the city.
"*Mira*," Abuela would say, pointing.

And I'd look, as we soared
over parks and streets, dogs and people.

We'd wave to the people waiting for the bus.
"*Buenos días*," we'd say.
"*Buenos días*. Good morning," they'd call up to us.
We'd fly over factories and trains . . .

and glide close to the sea.
"*Cerca del mar,*" we'd say.
We'd almost touch the tops of waves.

Abuela's skirt would be a sail.
She could race with the sailboats.
I'll bet she'd win.

We'd fly to where the ships are docked,
and watch people unload fruits
from the land where Abuela grew up.
Mangos, bananas, papayas—
those are all Spanish words.
So are rodeo, patio, and burro.
Maybe we'd see a cousin of Abuela's
hooking boxes of fruit to a crane.
We saw her cousin Daniel once,
unloading and loading the ships.

Out past the boats in the harbor
we'd see the Statue of Liberty.
"Me gusta," Abuela would say.
Abuela really likes her.
I do too.
We would circle around Liberty's head
and wave to the people visiting her.
That would remind Abuela of when
she first came to this country.

"*Vamos al aeropuerto,*" she'd say.
She'd take me to the airport where
the plane that first brought her landed.
"*Cuidado,*" Abuela would tell me.
We'd have to be careful
as we went for a short ride.

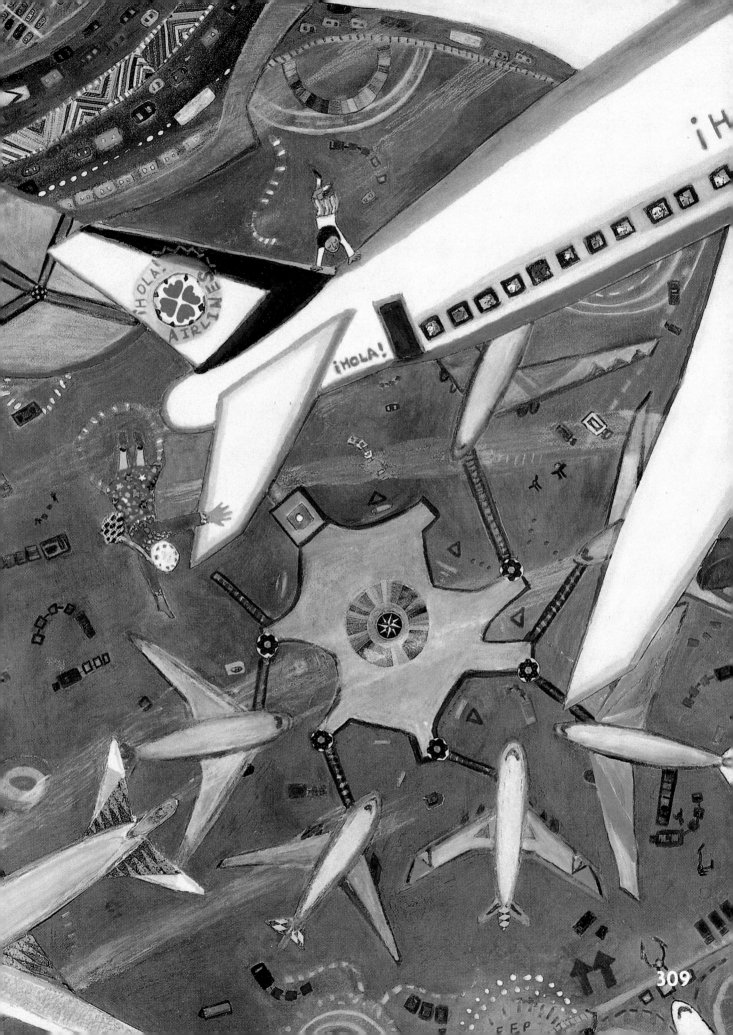

Then we could fly to *tío* Pablo's
and *tía* Elisa's store.
Pablo is my uncle, my *tío*,
and Elisa is my aunt, my *tía*.
They'd be surprised when we flew in,
but they'd offer us a cool *limonada*.
Flying is hot work.
"Pero quiero volar más,"
Abuela would say.
She wants to fly more.
I want to fly more too.

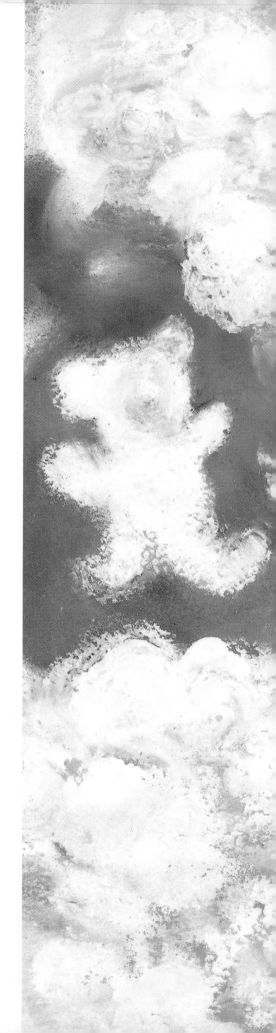

We could fly to *las nubes,* the clouds.
One looks like a cat, *un gato.*
One looks like a bear, *un oso.*
One looks like a chair, *una silla.*
"Descansemos un momento,"
Abuela would say.
She wants to rest a moment.
We would rest in our chair,
and Abuela would hold me in her arms,
with the whole sky
our house, *nuestra casa.*

We'd be as high as airplanes,
balloons, and birds,
and higher than the tall buildings downtown.
But we'd fly there too
to look around.

We could find the building
where my father works.
"*Hola, papá*," I'd say as I waved.
And Abuela would do a flip for fun
as we passed by the windows.

"*Mira,*" I hear Abuela say.

"Look," she's telling me.

I do look,
and we are back in the park.

We are walking by the lake.
Abuela probably wants to go for a boat ride.
"Vamos a otra aventura," she says.
She wants us to go for another adventure.
That's just one of the things I love
about Abuela.
She likes adventures.

Abuela takes my hand.
"*Vamos,*" she says.
"Let's go."

Glossary

Use this list to learn the Spanish words. Read the sounds that are next to the words. Then read the meanings.

Abuela (ah-BWEH-lah) Grandmother

Buenos días (BWEH-nohs DEE-ahs) Good day

Cerca del mar (SEHR-kah dehl mahr) Close to the sea

Cuidado (kwee-DAH-doh) Be careful

Descansemos un momento (dehs-kahn-SEH-mohs oon moh-MEHN-toh) Let's rest a moment

El parque es lindo (ehl PAHR-kay ehs LEEN-doh) The park is beautiful

Hola, papá (OH-lah, pah-PAH) Hello, papa

Las nubes (lahs NOO-behs) The clouds

Limonada (lee-moh-NAH-dah) Lemonade

Me gusta (meh GOO-stah) I like

Mira (MEE-rah) Look

Nuestra casa (NWEH-strah CAH-sah) Our house

Pero quiero volar más (PEH-roh key-EH-roh boh-LAR mahs) But I would like to fly more

Rosalba el pájaro (roh-SAHL-bah ehl PAH-hah-roh) Rosalba the bird

Sí, quiero volar (see, key-EH-roh boh-LAR) Yes, I want to fly

Tantos pájaros (TAHN-tohs PAH-hah-rohs) So many birds

Tía (TEE-ah) Aunt

Tío (TEE-oh) Uncle

Un gato (oon GAH-toh) A cat

Un oso (oon OH-soh) A bear

Una silla (OON-ah SEE-yah) A chair

Vamos (BAH-mohs) Let's go

Vamos al aeropuerto (BAH-mohs ahl ah-ehr-oh-PWEHR-toh) Let's go to the airport

Vamos a otra aventura (BAH-mohs ah OH-trah ah-behn-TOO-rah) Let's go on another adventure

Ven (behn) Come

In Response

Fly in the Sky Where would you like to fly? What things would you see? Draw a big picture of this place. Tell a classmate about it.

Speak Spanish With a partner, look in the glossary to read the Spanish words from the story. Practice saying them aloud.

Going Places Rosalba and her grandmother liked to go places together. Who do you like to go places with? Write a page about the person, and tell about the places you go.

DREAM SONG

A song of the Chippewa people

High in the sky I go,
walking in the sky I go,
high above the way below,
  way below.

By my side a bird will go,
bird and I above the way below,
  way below.

High across the sky I go,
walking with a bird I go,
all around the sky we go,
all around we go,
in the sky we go,
  bird and I.

Looking Through an Artist's Imagination

Art can show how an artist feels about the world. What is imaginative in these two pieces of art? How do these works make you use *your* imagination?

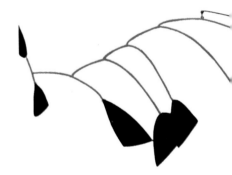

Paris Through the Window

Painting by Marc Chagall (Russian), 1913

Marc Chagall, Paris Through the Window (Paris par la fenetre). 1913,
Oil on canvas. 53 1/2 x 55 3/4 inches) Solomon R. Guggenheim Museum,
New York, Gift, Solomon R. Guggenheim, 1937 PHOTO: David Heald
© The Solomon R. Guggenheim Foundation, New York FN37.438.

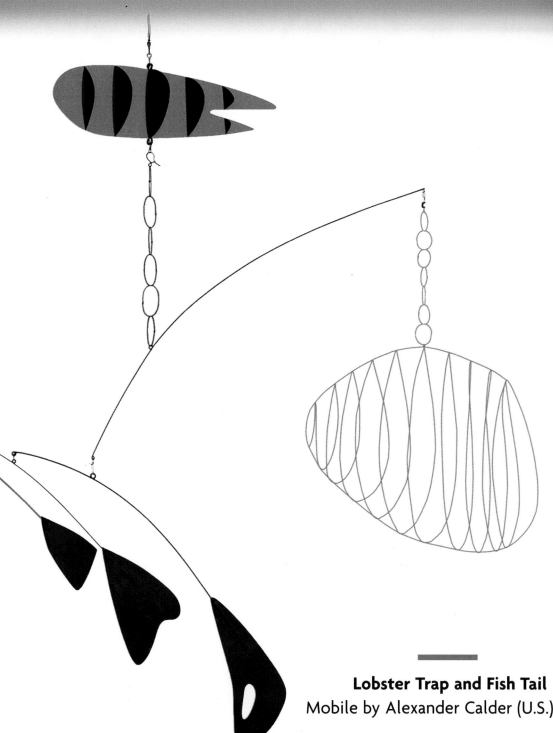

Lobster Trap and Fish Tail
Mobile by Alexander Calder (U.S.), 1939

Author and Illustrator at Work

Steven Kellogg nearly covered the walls of his room with drawings when he was young. He drew birds and animals. When he was older, he worked in a dog kennel. He used the money he earned to buy art supplies. He still likes animals. Today he walks in the woods with his Great Dane while he thinks about his stories.

★ Award-winning Book

Uncle McAllister lived in Scotland. Every year he sent Louis a birthday gift for his nature collection.

"This is the best one yet!" cried Louis.

The next day he took his entire collection to school for show-and-tell.

"Class, this is a tadpole," said Mrs. Shelbert. She asked Louis to bring it back often so they could all watch it become a frog.

Louis named the tadpole Alphonse. Every day Alphonse ate several cheeseburgers.

Louis found that he was eager to learn.

When Alphonse became too big for his jar, Louis moved him to the sink.

After Alphonse outgrew the sink, Louis's parents agreed to let him use the bathtub.

One day Mrs. Shelbert decided that Alphonse was not turning into an ordinary frog.

She asked Louis to stop bringing him to school.

By the time summer vacation arrived, Alphonse was enormous.

"He's too big for the bathtub," said Louis's mother.

"He's too big for the apartment," said Louis's father.

"He needs a swimming pool," said Louis.

"There is no place in our apartment for a swimming pool," said his parents.

Louis suggested that they buy the parking lot next door and build a swimming pool.

"It would cost more money than we have," said his parents. "Your tadpole will have to be donated to the zoo."

The thought of Alphonse in a cage made Louis very sad.

Then, in the middle of the night, Louis remembered that the junior high had a swimming pool that nobody used during the summer.

Louis hid Alphonse under a rug and smuggled him into the school.

After making sure that Alphonse felt at home, Louis went back to bed.

Every morning Louis spent several hours swimming with his friend. In the afternoon he earned the money for Alphonse's cheeseburgers by delivering newspapers.

Meanwhile the training continued. Alphonse learned to retrieve things from the bottom of the pool.

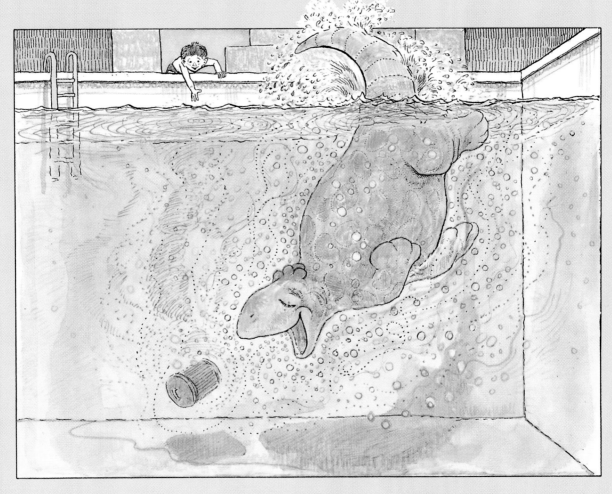

Summer vacation passed quickly. Louis worried what would happen to Alphonse now that school had reopened.

As soon as the first day ended, he ran to the junior high. The students were getting ready for after-school activities.

Louis arrived just as the first swimming race began.

Alphonse was delighted to see all the swimmers.

"It's a submarine from another planet!" bellowed the coach. "Call the police! Call the Navy!"

"No! It's a tadpole!" cried Louis. "He's my pet!"

The coach was upset and confused.

"You have until tomorrow," he cried, "to get that creature out of the pool!"

Louis didn't know what to do. On the way home he met his friend Miss Seevers, the librarian, and he told her his problem.

Miss Seevers went back to the junior high school with Louis, but when she saw Alphonse, she was so shocked that she dropped her purse and the books she was carrying into the swimming pool. Alphonse retrieved them.

Then Miss Seevers telephoned Louis's Uncle McAllister in Scotland. He told her that he had caught the little tadpole in Loch Ness, a large lake near his cottage.

Miss Seevers said, "I'm convinced that your uncle has given you a very rare Loch Ness monster!"

"I don't care!" cried Louis. "He's my pet, and I love him!"
He begged Miss Seevers to help him raise enough money to buy
the parking lot near his apartment so he could build a swimming
pool for Alphonse.

Suddenly Miss Seevers had an idea.

"In 1639 there was a battle in our city's harbor," she said.
"A pirate treasure ship was sunk, and no one has ever been able
to find it. But perhaps we can!"

The next morning Miss Seevers and Louis rented a boat.

In the middle of the harbor Louis showed Alphonse a picture of a treasure chest.

Alphonse disappeared under the water.

Louis and Miss Seevers bought the parking lot.

They hired some helpers.

And when the pool was completed,

all the children in the city were invited to swim.

That night Louis said, "Alphonse, next week is my birthday, which means that we've been friends for almost a year."

Far away in Scotland Uncle McAllister was also thinking about the approaching birthday. While out hiking he discovered an unusual stone in a clump of grass and sticks.

"A perfect gift for my nephew!" he cried.

"I'll deliver it in person!"

Uncle McAllister arrived at Louis's apartment and gave Louis the present.

Louis couldn't wait to add it to his collection.

Suddenly a crack appeared in the stone. . . .

In Response

 Bird Watching What happens after Louis's bird hatches from the egg? With a partner, make up more of the story.

 Tadpole Stories How would Louis's parents have told the story of the mysterious tadpole? With a friend, pretend you are Louis's parents and tell what happened.

 Mystery Pets If you could have a mysterious pet, what would it look like? Draw a picture and write about it. Tell the things you and your pet would do.

The Mysterious
NESSIE

For hundreds of years, people have noticed something huge and strange swimming in Loch Ness, a deep lake in Scotland. Some call it a "beastie." Others call it Nessie—the Loch Ness monster.

Is Nessie real? To find out, divers have hunted the deep, dark waters. People have offered Nessie bait—and even piano music! But Nessie has not appeared.

People have taken pictures of Nessie—but the pictures aren't very clear. The best one was taken in 1934. Sixty years later, a man admitted it was a picture of a toy submarine with a plastic neck!

Some people say Nessie is only a wave, or a floating log, or a huge fish. Others still say that, somewhere in Loch Ness, a mysterious creature is hiding.

Theme Trade Books

Alistair and the Alien Invasion

by Marilyn Sadler, illustrated by Roger Bollen, Silver Burdett Ginn, 1996

Alistair Grittle, boy genius, sets out in his spaceship to find the most unusual plant for his science project. On his way he sees aliens landing on Earth and decides to spy on them. When his adventure is over, Alistair has made new friends, saved the earth, and received a special present.

Sitting in My Box

by Dee Lillegard, illustrated by Jon Agee, Silver Burdett Ginn, 1996

A boy sits alone in a box reading. A tall giraffe asks to join him, and the boy lets him in. Soon the box is filled with animals. When the animals won't leave, the boy gets help from a tiny flea.

More Books for You to Enjoy

There Was Magic Inside
by David Galchutt, Simon & Schuster, 1993

Soon after a young boy finds a box full of magic things, he has to use what's in the box to fight a terrible dragon.

Dogs Don't Wear Sneakers
by Laura Numeroff, illustrated by Joe Mathieu, Simon & Schuster, 1993

Everyone knows that a dog doesn't wear sneakers, but anything is possible when you use your imagination.

Guys from Space
by Daniel Pinkwater, Macmillan, 1989

When a spaceship lands on Earth, a little boy gets to take an outer space tour and visits a planet that has a root beer stand.

357

Glossary

acorn

braid

cartwheel

A

acorn A nut, or fruit, of an oak tree. An *acorn* fell off the tree.

abandoned Left behind, not in use. The windows of the old, *abandoned* house were broken.

alley Narrow street behind buildings. We found empty boxes in the *alley* behind the store.

B

band A strip that is put around something. The bird has a *band* on its leg.

beach Sand and pebbles next to a sea or lake. We sat on the *beach* looking at the lake.

bellow To shout loudly. The police officer *bellowed* for the car to stop.

braid Hair that has been woven together. She wore her long black hair in two *braids*.

C

cartwheel A trick done by putting your hands down and swinging your feet overhead. She did a handstand and a *cartwheel*.

ceiling The top part of a room. The light on the *ceiling* wasn't working.

charming Very pleasing. The little boy has a *charming* smile.

coop A cage for birds or other small animals. They put the chickens in a *coop*.

crabby Grouchy or in a bad mood. When I'm very tired or mad, I am the *crabbiest* person in my family.

crate A box made of wood. The *crate* was filled with oranges.

creature Any person or animal is a creature. I saw a bear and another big *creature* in the woods.

curious Wanting to know. People who are *curious* ask many questions.

curl To bend or roll up. The little puppy liked to *curl* up next to its mother.

customer A person who buys something. The *customer* paid a dime for a pencil.

daily Happening every day. I took the dog for its *daily* walk.

disappoint To not do something wanted or hoped for. I did not want to *disappoint* my friends by not going to the party.

coop

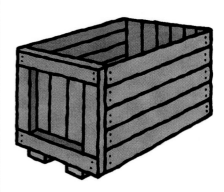

crate

curl

empty

flip

flour

dough A mixture made mostly of flour and water. When we make bread, Dad mixes the *dough*.

earn To get paid for work that has been done. The workers *earn* ten dollars each hour.

empty Having nothing in it. The bottle of milk was *empty*.

enormous Very big. It was the most *enormous* cookie I had ever seen.

expensive Having a high price. The new car was very *expensive*.

flap To move with a slapping sound. The flag was *flapping* in the wind.

flip A quick turning over in the air. My sister taught me how to do back *flips*.

flour A powder made of wheat that is used to bake foods. You need *flour* to make bread.

gently In a gentle way; softly. She held the puppy *gently* in her arms.

glide To move in a smooth way. It's fun to *glide* across the ice on ice skates.

golden Having a yellow color. I colored the lion a pretty *golden* color like the sun.

golden

harbor A place near land where ships can be safely tied up. The boat sailed into the *harbor.*

hike To take a long walk. We went *hiking* up that tall mountain.

hornet A large flying insect that can sting. We did not go near the *hornet's* nest.

hum To sing with the lips closed, not saying any words. She didn't remember the words to the song, but she could *hum* the tune.

hike

information Facts. You can look in this book to get *information* for your report.

inspection A careful check. Our workshop had to pass a safety *inspection.*

instinct A way of acting that is natural to an animal. Birds don't have to be taught to build nests—they do it by *instinct.*

**hornet
(a Vespa hornet)**

knead

lumber

lumpy

J

jazz A kind of music first played by African Americans. *Jazz* singers often make up the words to songs as they are singing.

junior high A school between elementary school and high school. After I finish elementary school, I will go to the *junior high*.

K

knead To press and squeeze something over and over. The bakers *knead* the dough before they make it into a loaf of bread.

knit To sew with needles and yarn. She was *knitting* a pair of red socks.

L

librarian A person who works in a library. The *librarian* was putting new books on the library shelves.

lumber Wood that has been sawed into boards. The trees were cut down and made into *lumber*.

lumpy Full of bumps. It was hard to sleep because the bed was *lumpy*.

M

machine Something made of parts that does some type of work. In the building, they had five washing *machines*.

mail Letters and packages that are sent to a person or place. There was a big pile of *mail* on the desk.

mango A sweet fruit that is yellow and red. The *mangoes* tasted very sweet.

matter Trouble or something that is wrong. The boy looks unhappy, so something must be the *matter*.

migratory Moving long distances. Birds that fly south for the winter are *migratory*.

musician A person who knows how to make music. The young *musician* is playing a clarinet.

N

nephew The son of a person's brother or sister. My aunts sent a birthday present to their *nephew*.

niece The daughter of a person's brother or sister. The *niece* visited her aunt and uncle.

ninety A counting number written as 90. I counted *ninety* marbles in the jar.

mail

migratory

musician

ocean

package

peck

notice To see. His friends did not *notice* his new haircut.

ocean A large body of salt water. Whales live in the *ocean*.

ordinary What you're used to; not different. It was an *ordinary* coat that looked just like the one I wore last year.

package A box with something packed in it. The children opened the surprise *package*.

paperwork Work done on paper. Every Saturday night, she pays the bills, writes letters, and does other *paperwork*.

peck To pick at something the way a bird does with its beak. The birds will *peck* on a piece of bread until it is gone.

picky Finding little things wrong. The *picky* cook thought the soup was too salty.

pinch To squeeze with two fingers. Grandpa *pinched* my cheek when he saw me.

pod A shell that holds seeds. Peas grow in a *pod*.

purse A small bag for carrying things. She put her money in her *purse*.

purse

R

rare Not often found or seen. There are only two of these *rare* coins in the world.

raspberry A small, juicy, red, purple or black fruit. She picked *raspberries* off the bush and ate them.

raspberry

refrigerator A machine in which the air is kept very cool so food will not go bad. He took a cold apple out of the *refrigerator*.

rescue To save from danger. She *rescued* a little duck that had broken its wing.

restaurant A place where people buy and eat meals. You can eat dinner with your family in a *restaurant*.

retrieve To find and bring back. If you throw the ball, my dog will *retrieve* it.

S

secret Something not known by others. She did not tell anyone my *secret*.

slurp To eat or drink in a noisy way. The baby pig made a mess as it *slurped* its food.

refrigerator

365

soar

swoop

towel

smuggle To bring or take in a secret way. We *smuggled* her surprise present into the house.

sneak To move or act in a secret way. They *sneaked* out of the room and then ran out the door.

soar To fly high in the air. The plane *soared* over the house tops.

stroke To pet in a gentle way. He *strokes* the dog's head after it does a trick.

sunrise The time when the sun comes up each morning. If you want to see the sun come up in the morning, you have to get up at *sunrise*.

sunset The time when the sun goes down each evening. The sun disappears behind the mountains at *sunset*.

surprise Something that you do not expect to happen. My uncle does not know about the *surprise* party we are planning for his birthday.

swoop To dive down through the air. The kite came *swooping* down from the sky.

T

together With one another. The two friends always did their homework *together*.

towel A large piece of cloth used for drying. We hung two new *towels* near the bathtub.

treasure Things that are valuable or are important. I put all the things I liked best in a *treasure* box.

unfamiliar Not known well. I heard an *unfamiliar* voice call my name.

usual Happening most of the time. As *usual*, we will go to the movies on Saturday.

vacation A break from work or school. I like to go swimming when I am on summer *vacation*.

warm Not cool but not hot. I don't like hot soup, but I like it *warm*.

windowsill The piece of wood at the bottom of a window. I put the plant on the *windowsill* so that it would be in the sunlight.

warm

windowsill

ACKNOWLEDGMENTS

Grateful acknowledgment is made to the following publishers, authors, and agents for their permission to reprint copyrighted material. Every effort has been made to locate all copyright proprietors; any errors or omissions in copyright notice are inadvertent and will be corrected in future printings as they are discovered.

Abuela by Arthur Dorros. Illustrated by Elisa Kleven. Text copyright ©1991 by Arthur Dorros. Illustrations copyright ©1991 by Elisa Kleven. Used by permission of Dutton Children's Books, a division of Penguin Books USA Inc.

A Birthday Basket for Tía by Pat Mora. Illustrated by Cecily Lang. Text copyright ©1992 by Pat Mora. Reprinted with permission of Macmillan Books for Young Readers, Simon & Schuster Children's Publishing Division.

"Buddies" from *Under the Sunday Tree* by Eloise Greenfield. Painting by Amos Ferguson. Text copyright ©1988 by Eloise Greenfield. Painting copyright ©1988 by Amos Ferguson. Reprinted by permission of HarperCollins Publishers and the author's agent.

"Cousins Are Cozy" from *Fathers, Mothers, Sisters, Brothers: A Collection of Family Poems* by Mary Ann Hoberman. Text copyright ©1991 by Mary Ann Hoberman. Reprinted by permission of Little, Brown and Company.

Dear Mr. Blueberry by Simon James. Copyright ©1991 by Simon James. Reprinted with permission of the American publisher, Margaret McElderry Books, Simon & Schuster Children's Publishing Division, and the British publisher, Walker Books Limited.

"Dream Song" from *Songs of The Chippewa* by John Bierhorst, adapted from the collections of Frances Densmore and Henry Rowe Schoolcraft. Copyright ©1974 by John Bierhorst. Reprinted by permission of the author.

"Fambly Time" from *Night on Neighborhood Street* by Eloise Greenfield. Copyright ©1991 by Eloise Greenfield. Used by permission of Dial Books for Young Readers, a division of Penguin Books USA Inc.

"A friend is someone who answers your...." from *I Need All the Friends I Can Get* by Charles M. Schulz. ©1964, 1981 by United Feature Syndicate, Inc. **Peanuts** reprinted by permission of UFS, Inc.

"A friend is someone who eats lunch...." from *I Need All the Friends I Can Get* by Charles M. Schulz. ©1964, 1981 by United Feature Syndicate, Inc. **Peanuts** reprinted by permission of UFS, Inc.

"A friend is someone who makes you...." from *I Need All the Friends I Can Get* by Charles M. Schulz. ©1964, 1981 by United Feature Syndicate, Inc. **Peanuts** reprinted by permission of UFS, Inc.

Home in the Sky story and pictures by Jeannie Baker. Copyright ©1984 by Jeannie Baker. Reprinted by permission of Greenwillow Books, a division of William Morrow & Company, Inc.

Julius story by Angela Johnson. Pictures by Dav Pilkey. Text copyright ©1993 by Angela Johnson. Illustrations copyright ©1993 by Dav Pilkey. Reprinted by permission of Orchard Books, New York.

"The Letter" from *Frog and Toad Are Friends* by Arnold Lobel. Copyright ©1970 by Arnold Lobel. Reprinted by permission of the American publisher, HarperCollins Publisher, and the British publisher, William Heinemann Ltd.

Little Nino's Pizzeria by Karen Barbour. Copyright ©1987 by Karen Barbour. Reprinted by permission of Harcourt Brace & Company.

"Looking Around" from *Out in the Dark and Daylight* by Aileen Fisher. Text copyright ©1980 by Aileen Fisher. Reprinted by permission of the author.

Matthew and Tilly by Rebecca C. Jones. Illustrated by Beth Peck. Text copyright ©1991 by Rebecca C. Jones. Illustrations copyright ©1991 by Beth Peck. Used by permission of Dutton Children's Books, a division of Penguin Books USA Inc.

The Mysterious Tadpole by Steven Kellogg. Copyright ©1977 by Steven Kellogg. Used by permission of the American publisher, Dial Books for Young Readers, a division of Penguin Books USA Inc., and the British agent, Sheldon Fogelman.

Nature Spy by Shelley Rotner and Ken Kreisler. Illustrations by Shelley Rotner. Text copyright ©1992 by Shelley Rotner and Ken Kreisler. Illustrations copyright ©1992 by Shelley Rotner. Reprinted with permission of Macmillan Books for Young Readers, Simon & Schuster Children's Publishing Division.

Phonetic respelling system from *The World Book Encyclopedia*. ©1995 World Book, Inc. By permission of the publisher.

Truman's Aunt Farm written by Jama Kim Rattigan and illustrated by G. Brian Karas. Text copyright ©1994 by Jama Kim Rattigan. Illustrations copyright ©1994 by G. Brian Karas. Reprinted by permission of Houghton Mifflin Co. All rights reserved.

"Why Ants Live Everywhere" from *How the People Sang the Mountains Up* by Maria Leach. Copyright ©1967 by Maria Leach. Used by permission of Viking Penguin, a division of Penguin Books USA Inc.

"Zuni Grandmother" from *Grandparents' Houses: Poems about Grandparents* selected by Corrine Streich. Collection copyright ©1984 by Corrine Streich. Used by permission of Mews Books, Ltd.

COVER: Cover Photography, © 1996 by Jade Albert Studio. Cover Illustration, © 1996 by Jurg Obrist. Cover design, art direction and production by Design Five.

ILLUSTRATION: 4–5, Nancy Coffelt (top bar); 6–7, Gerardo Suzan (top bar); 8–9, Tungwai Chau (top bar); 10–11, Nancy Coffelt; 60, Paula Cohen (all); 90–91, Susan Keeter; 120–121, Nancy Coffelt (border); Cristine Mortenson (background); 122, Gerardo Suzan; 136, Shelley Rotner; 156, Gerardo Suzan; 157, James Chaffee (border); 218–219, Cristine Mortenson (background); Gerardo Suzan (border); 220, Tungwai Chau; 284, David Johnson; 286, David Johnson; 323, Terry Widener; 355, Mark Steele; 356–357, Cristine Mortenson (background); Tungwai Chau (border); 358–367, Sudi McCullum.

PHOTOGRAPHY: Unless otherwise indicated, photographs of book covers were provided by Ulsaker Studio, Inc. Background photograph for Silver Bookcase by Allan Penn for SBG. The abbreviation SBG stands for Silver Burdett Ginn. Photo styling for selection openers provided by Anne Bugatch and Lance Salemo. All Fine Art Portfolio frames by Allan Penn for SBG. 12, Courtesy of Rebecca Jones (t.); Courtesy of Beth Peck (b.); 12–13, George Disario for SBG; 39, Doug Mindell for SBG; 41 George Disario for SBG (both); 42, George Disario for SBG (b.); 44, Courtesy of HarperCollins (t.l.); 44–45, Allan Penn for SBG; 61, Courtesy of John McLaughlin (t.); 62, Courtesy of Harcourt Brace & Company (t.l.); 62–63, Doug Mindell for SBG; 92, Hampton University Museum, Hampton, Virginia (l.); 92–93, Private Collection, New York/The Bridgeman Art Library, London; 94, Courtesy of Pat Mora (t.); Courtesy of Cecily Lang (b.); 94–95, Allan Penn for SBG; 118, © 1994 Lee Marmon (b.l.); 118–119, Allan Penn for SBG; 119, George Disario for SBG (t.r.); 124, Courtesy of Shelley Rotner (t.); Courtesy of Ken Kreisler (b.); 124–125, George Disario for SBG; 126–152, Shelley Rotner (all); 153, Shelley Rotner (t.); Doug Mindell for SBG (c., b.); 154, Courtesy of El Museo del Barrio, NY (l.); 154–155, Collection of Chuck and Jan Rosenak, Photo: Lynn Lown; 157, George Disario for SBG (c.); 158, Courtesy of William Morrow & Company (t.l.); 158–159, Allan Penn for SBG; 190, Courtesy of Walker Books, Ltd. (t.l.); 190–191, Allan Penn for SBG; 216–217, © David E. Myers/Tony Stone Images; 222, Courtesy of Orchard Books (both); 222–223, Doug Mindell for SBG; 253, Daniel Hyland (both); 254, Courtesy of Jama Kim Rattigan (t.); Courtesy of G. Brian Karas (b.); 254–255, Allan Penn for SBG; 288, Courtesy of Arthur Dorros (t.); Clair Wigfall, courtesy of Elisa Kleven (b.); 288–289, Allan Penn for SBG; 324–325, Calder, Alexander. *Lobster Trap and Fish Tail.* (1939). Hanging mobile: painted steel wire and sheet aluminum, about 8'6"h. x 9'6" diam. (260 x 290 cm). The Museum of Modern Art, New York. Commissioned by the Advisory Committee for the stairwell of the Museum. Photograph © 1995 The Museum of Modern Art, New York.; 326, Courtesy of Penguin USA; 326–327, Lou Goodman for SBG; 354, Doug Mindell for SBG (b.); 355, AP/Wide World Photos (l.); photo of 3-D Illustration by Allan Penn for SBG (r.); 358, Doug Mindell for SBG (t.); 361, © J. H. Robinson/Photo Researchers, Inc. (b.); 362, © Chromasohm/Sohm/AllStock (c.); 363, © Scott Nielsen/Bruce Coleman, Inc. (c.); 364, © Jeff Foott/DRK Photo (t.).